ELECTIONS
Choosing Our Leaders

Paul Bamaton

The Rosen Publishing Group's
PowerKids Press™
New York

Published in 2009 by The Rosen Publishing Group, Inc.
29 East 21st Street, New York, NY 10010

Copyright © 2009 by The Rosen Publishing Group, Inc.

Book Design: Michael J. Flynn

Photo Credits: Cover, p. 13 © Digital Vision/Getty Images; p. 5 © Lisa F. Young/Shutterstock; p. 6 ©
Christina Ciochina/Shutterstock; p. 9 © Kasia/Shutterstock; p. 10 © Alexey Stiop/Shutterstock; p. 18 ©
Jorge Salcedo/Shutterstock; p. 21 © Tim Sloan/AFP/Getty Images; p. 22 © Tomasz Trojanowski/Shutterstock.

Library of Congress Cataloging-in-Publication Data

Bamaton, Paul.
  Elections : choosing our leaders / Paul Bamaton.
      p. cm. - (Real life readers)
  Includes index.
  ISBN: 978-1-4358-0084-7 (pbk.)
  6-pack ISBN: 978-1-4358-0088-5
  ISBN: 978-1-4358-2979-4 (library binding)
  1. Elections-United States-Juvenile literature. 2. Representative government and representation-United States-
Juvenile literature. I. Title.
  JK1978.B36 2009
  324.60973-dc22
                                        2008036703

Manufactured in the United States of America

Contents

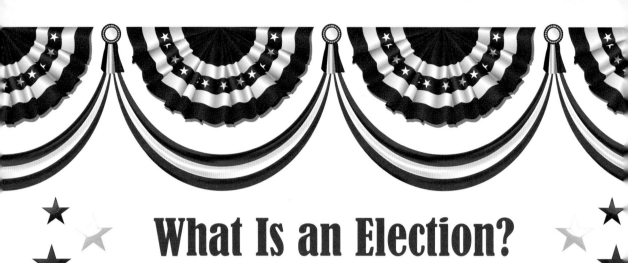

What Is an Election?

Did you ever wonder how the people who make the rules and laws we live by are chosen? We hold elections. An election is a system that allows citizens to choose the people who will become their **representatives** in the government.

In some places, people vote with paper **ballots**. In other places, they use machines to **cast** their votes. Every vote is cast in private. On election days, people vote in special places called polling places. The polling places usually open early in the morning and close late in the evening to make sure everyone has a chance to vote.

In most cases, the winner of an election is the person who receives the most votes—the person chosen by the majority of the voters to officially represent them.

This man is touching a computer screen to cast his vote.

This is the U.S. Capitol in Washington, D.C.
Congress, the legislative branch of the federal government,
meets here to make laws.

Elected Officials

In the United States, we elect representatives for the **executive**, **legislative**, and **judicial** branches of government. These three branches can be found at national, state, and local levels. They work separately and together at each level to make and carry out laws.

Each branch has different jobs and **responsibilities**. The executive branch is the leader of the country, state, or community and directs laws. The legislative branch makes laws. The judicial branch, which is made up of the courts, explains and applies laws.

Our nation's **Constitution** tells the responsibilities of the national government and the powers that belong to the states. Each state also has its own constitution listing its responsibilities. The states then give certain responsibilities to their local governments.

A Voice in the Government

Our Constitution states how the government should work. It tells the rights, responsibilities, and duties of the government as well as the rights, responsibilities, and duties of the people.

The United States is a **representative democracy**. This means that people elect leaders who will represent them in making laws and running the government. Through voting, people decide who they think will best represent their interests, ideas, needs, and concerns. If people are unhappy with the way an official does their job, they can vote for someone else in the next election.

This picture shows the words that begin the U.S. Constitution. The Constitution was written in 1787.

This town hall is where local leaders meet
to make the laws for their community.

Local Government

Officials in all branches of government are responsible to the citizens who elect them. What governing powers does a local government have in its community?

We know that local governments have responsibilities given to them by the state. These responsibilities are based on the needs and wants of the communities they serve. That is why the powers and responsibilities of all local governments aren't the same.

A local government may serve a village, town, city, or county. Some areas have more than one local government. For example, a city or town may have a **municipal** government and a county government. Each of these governments has different responsibilities.

The responsibilities of the executive, legislative, and judicial branches of local governments deal mostly with the everyday life of their citizens. They make, carry out, and apply local laws. Since local communities and governments aren't all the same, they may have different rules and laws and may be set up differently.

Leaders of local governments may be mayors, managers, or commissioners. Legislative bodies, made up of a few or many members, make the rules for the community. Local judges control the court system.

A community's local leader often speaks at community events.

Authority and Services

Do you know what services your local government provides? Local governments provide many services to the citizens of the community. They have the authority to tax the community to pay for these services. They also have the responsibility to prepare and adopt a plan that shows citizens what services will be provided and how much they will cost.

All communities have some needs in common. However, each community also has its own special needs. The services a community needs depend on such things as its population, size, location, and **economy**.

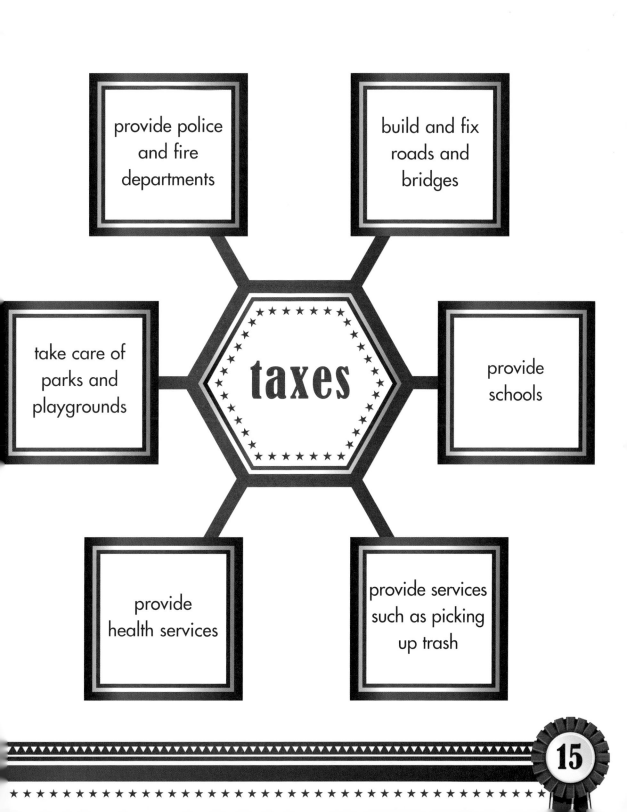

provide police and fire departments

build and fix roads and bridges

take care of parks and playgrounds

taxes

provide schools

provide health services

provide services such as picking up trash

What Is a Citizen?

A U.S. citizen is a person who is born in this country or who is born to parents who are U.S. citizens. A person can become a U.S. citizen by applying for citizenship and promising to be **loyal** to the United States.

U.S. citizens have rights, responsibilities, and duties under the law. They have rights such as the freedom to speak about their ideas and the freedom to write what they believe. They have responsibilities such as obeying laws and respecting the rights of others. Their duties include learning about matters that concern the public and voting in order to have a voice in how they are governed.

Can you think of other rights, responsibilities, and duties that citizens have?

RESPONSIBILITIES

- obeying the laws
- respecting the rights of others

RIGHTS

- freedom to speak and write ideas

DUTIES

- voting
- learning about public matters

CITIZENS

Some people join and march together to let others know how they feel about candidates and their ideas.

The Right to Vote

Our Constitution gives every citizen over the age of 18 the right to vote. This is one of the most important rights we have as citizens. It applies to citizens of all races and to both men and women. In many countries, people don't have this right.

When we vote, we choose the people whose ideas will direct our future. **Candidates** running for office tell us their ideas, plans, and beliefs. When we vote, we make judgments on how closely their thoughts and feelings match our own.

Voting in free and fair elections gives us control over how we are governed. Why do you think voting is important?

Making a Difference

In a democracy, voting isn't just a right—it's also a duty! When we vote, we make choices. We choose our leaders and show them the direction we want them to take. Voting gives us some control over our political system. Voting protects our rights as citizens.

People who don't vote allow others to decide who represents them. They let others decide how they're governed. They allow others to establish the rules and laws they live by.

Don't ever let anyone tell you that your vote doesn't matter. Each vote makes a difference!

The U.S. Congress has over 500 elected officials who make the laws for all the people of our nation. The people in Congress represent you!

The leaders we elect make a difference in the way the government runs. To make sure that everyone's interests are considered, citizens should have knowledge about who is running for office. The Internet can be a good way to learn about candidates and their ideas.

Knowing what a candidate believes helps us vote for the person we think will best use their authority and power to benefit everyone they represent.

Can you think of some ways you could learn about candidates before you vote?

This person uses a computer to find facts about candidates and their ideas.

Glossary

ballot (BA-luht) A printed sheet used in voting.

candidate (KAN-duh-dayt) A person who runs for an office.

cast (KAST) To record.

constitution (kahn-stuh-TOO-shun) The written beliefs and laws of a government.

economy (ih-KAH-nuh-mee) How money and goods are used.

executive (ig-ZEH-kyoo-tihv) The leader of a community or nation.

judicial (joo-DIH-shul) Having to do with the courts.

legislative (LEH-juhs-lay-tihv) Having the power to make laws.

loyal (LOHY-uhl) Faithful.

municipal (myoo-NIH-suh-puhl) Having to do with the government of a town or city.

representative (reh-prih-ZEHN-tuh-tihv) A person who acts for others.

representative democracy (reh-prih-ZEHN-tuh-tihv dih-MAH-kruh-see) A government where the people elect representatives to act for them.

responsibility (rih-spahn-suh-BIH-luh-tee) A duty.

 # Index

Due to the changing nature of Internet links, The Rosen Publishing Group, Inc., has developed an online list of Web sites related to the subject of this book. This site is updated regularly. Please use this link to access the list: http://www.rcbmlinks.com/rlr/elch